C

My Military Parent

Julie Murray

Abdo Kids Junior
is an Imprint of Abdo Kids
abdobooks.com

Abdo

THIS IS MY FAMILY

Kids

abdobooks.com

Published by Abdo Kids, a division of ABDO, P.O. Box 398166, Minneapolis, Minnesota 55439.
Copyright © 2021 by Abdo Consulting Group, Inc. International copyrights reserved in all countries.
No part of this book may be reproduced in any form without written permission from the publisher.
Abdo Kids Junior™ is a trademark and logo of Abdo Kids.

Printed in the United States of America, North Mankato, Minnesota.

052020

092020

THIS BOOK CONTAINS
RECYCLED MATERIALS

Photo Credits: iStock, Shutterstock, US Air Force, US Army, US Coast Guard, US Marines, US Navy,
©US Army Garrison Casey p.22 / CC BY-NC-ND 2.0, ©Coast Guard News p.22 / CC BY-NC-ND 2.0,
©US Pacific Fleet p.22 / CC BY-NC 2.0

Production Contributors: Teddy Borth, Jennie Forsberg, Grace Hansen

Design Contributors: Candice Keimig, Pakou Moua, Dorothy Toth

Library of Congress Control Number: 2019955594

Publisher's Cataloging-in-Publication Data

Names: Murray, Julie, author.

Title: My military parent / by Julie Murray

Description: Minneapolis, Minnesota : Abdo Kids, 2021 | Series: This is my family | Includes online
    resources and index.

Identifiers: ISBN 9781098202224 (lib. bdg.) | ISBN 9781644943908 (pbk.) | ISBN 9781098203207 (ebook)
    | ISBN 9781098203696 (Read-to-Me ebook)

Subjects: LCSH: Families--Juvenile literature. | Families of military personnel--Juvenile literature. |
    Children of military personnel--Juvenile literature. | Parent and child--Juvenile literature. | Families—
    Social aspects--Juvenile literature.

Classification: DDC 306.85--dc23

Table of Contents

My Military Parent

Some kids have parents who are in the military.

Mary's dad is in the Air Force.

He flies planes.

Zach's mom is in the Navy.

She works on a boat.

Ellen's mom is in the Marines.

She works hard!

Sometimes military families have to be apart. They video chat.

Sam's dad is in the Army.

He is going on **deployment**.

Lei's mom is in the
Coast Guard.

Sara is **proud** of her mom!

She received an award.

Luke is happy. His dad is home!

More Military Families

Air Force

Coast Guard

Marines

Army

Navy

Glossary

deployment
the movement of troops away from home to a place for military action and service.

military
the armed forces of a country.

proud
feeling pleased with and having respect for something someone has done.

23

Index

Abdo Kids
ONLINE
FREE! ONLINE MULTIMEDIA RESOURCES

Visit **abdokids.com**
to access crafts, games,
videos, and more!

Use Abdo Kids code
TMK2224
or scan this QR code!